10

Perfect Ideas For A Romantic Valentine's Day

By

Floyd B. Pung

Copyright © {2022} Floyd B. Pung

"You just need a little ingenuity and some extra work to make Valentine's Day memorable for the person you care about. Make it matter, and make it something you won't forget! Have fun!"

10

Perfect Ideas For A Romantic Valentine's Day

TABLLE OF CONTENTS

Introduction

On Valentine's Day, married people celebrate their love and admiration for one another while exchanging gifts and exchanging cards. There are a lot of fun and romantic things you can do to show your significant other how much you care, regardless of how long you've been together or how recently you've started a relationship with them. Here are ten wonderful suggestions for a romantic Valentine's Day that are sure to win over the heart of your partner. These suggestions will assist you in making this Valentine's Day one that will stand out in your mind, whether you want to have a quiet night in or embark on a weekend adventure with your significant other.

There are a lot of different ways to display love, from preparing a home-cooked meal for your significant other to take them on an adventure in a hot air balloon. There is something enjoyable for everyone, whether your idea of a good time is a cozy night in with your significant other, an exciting excursion in the great outdoors, or something a little more extravagant.

These ten suggestions for a romantic Valentine's Day will help you make this day memorable in a way that is meaningful to you and your significant other, whether your goal is to plan an unforgettable trip, plan a romantic evening at home, or find a unique way to surprise your partner with a unique gift. Get an early start on your preparations if you want this Valentine's Day to be the most romantic and special one yet.

You and that special someone are sure to have a Valentine's Day that is full of love and passion if you use any of these 10 great ideas. You will both remember this Valentine's Day with a fondness for many years to come.

Phase 1

Wonderful Suggestions for Making Valentine's Day Extra Romantic

Valentine's Day is a time for love and passion, and it's the perfect opportunity to tell that special someone how much they mean to you. It is essential to do something memorable for the person you spend the most time with on a daily basis. This could be as simple as a candlelit supper for two or as elaborate as a weekend getaway.

Have a charming breakfast in bed to get the day started off right. Cook your significant other's favorite dish and serve it to them besides a single red rose. After that, take a stroll through a park or along the ocean to continue the romantic atmosphere. To help you remember the day and the precious moments you shared together, take pictures.

In the evening, create an intimate atmosphere by lighting candles, playing music, and serving a delectable meal. Create a memorable evening by cooking a romantic meal complete with a bottle of wine and a delectable dessert. Prepare the meal using your most elegant china, and dress to make an impression.

After dinner, you and your guests can unwind together in the hot tub or go for a walk outside under the night sky. Make sure that whatever you do, is something that the two of you can enjoy doing together, no matter what it is.

Last but not least, finish the evening off with a lovely present. Choose an item that represents the two of you and is unique to the two of you alone, such as a piece of jewelry, a photo album, or a unique keepsake.

Make sure that however you choose to celebrate Valentine's Day, the day is memorable for the person you share an important relationship with. Spend the day being romantic, demonstrating your love for one another, and making memorable experiences.

1. Have a Barbecue or Picnic

Valentine's Day is a beautiful occasion filled with love, passion, and spending quality time with the person you cherish the most. A picnic is a fun and different way to spend the day if you're searching for something different to do during the day. It is a wonderful way to celebrate Valentine's Day to get together with your loved one, prepare a picnic basket, and go to a nearby park or beach to take in each other's company.

Make sure you have enough of all the necessary items for your picnic before you leave. It is essential to bring along a blanket for sitting on, some food and drinks, as well as possibly some additional supplies such as plates, silverware, and napkins. When you have everything you need, look for a pleasant place to have your picnic and set it up. If you're in the mood for some excitement, you could even go on a trek and find a secluded spot to have a picnic.

When it comes to eating, there is a virtually infinite variety of options. There are many delicious options available, including fruits, salads, wraps, and sandwiches. You may also make some sweet snacks, like cookies and cupcakes, if you want to make the day even more memorable than it already is. Don't forget to bring some drinks with you so you can flush everything down.

After you've finished eating and found a comfortable spot, there are a few things you can do to make your picnic even more intimate. Even if all you do is talk to one another and cuddle up close, the day will feel even more special if you play games like badminton or frisbee with each other. You can put the cherry on top of the day by ending it with a romantic stroll while the sun is setting.

On Valentine's Day, treating your significant other to a picnic is a wonderful way to express your affection and gratitude for them. You and your significant other are able to organize and put together the elements of an unforgettable and passionate day with only a little bit of effort, which you will both come to appreciate and remember fondly for many years to come.

2. Schedule a night to watch movies.

On Valentine's Day, couples, friends, and family members all join together to share their love for one another and celebrate the holiday. A night in front of the television with some popcorn and romantic flicks is an excellent way to mark the occasion. A Valentine's Day movie night may be a fun and memorable experience for everyone engaged in the event, especially if you plan it ahead of time.

The selection of films to view during a movie night should be the first step taken when organizing such an event. On Valentine's Day, romantic comedies are almost always a big hit, so picking out a handful of your favourites is a wonderful place to get started.

You might also choose to watch one or two older romantic films from the past in order to add a touch of sentimentality to the evening. After settling on the films to watch, the next step is to select a time and location for the viewing. It might take place in the living room of your home, at the home of a friend, or even in a movie theater.

The next thing you need to do is check that you have all of the necessary tools. You will require a television, a player capable of playing DVDs or Blu-rays, and speakers. In most cases, if you are watching a film at a theater, the theater will provide all of the necessary equipment for you. Check to see that there is sufficient seating for all of the guests who will be attending the movie night.

The selection of food is another essential component in organizing a movie night. The traditional go-to snack for movie nights is popcorn, but you can also make the evening more memorable by serving candy, chips, cookies, and other delights in addition to popcorn. You might also offer beverages such as soda, juice, or even hot cocoa to your guests.

Last but not least, you need to organize something fun to do after the movie. This could take the form of having a conversation, playing a board game, or simply taking pleasure in each other's company.

On Valentine's Day, it can be a wonderful opportunity to gather together the people you care about and create memories that will last a lifetime if you organize a movie night. You just need the appropriate amount of planning to pull off a night at the movies that are both romantic and pleasant for everyone involved.

3. Exchange Personalized Gifts

On Valentine's Day, it's important to let individuals you care about know how much you cherish and value your relationship with them. Exchanging one another with personalized presents is one of the most common strategies to accomplish this goal. Because of their thoughtfulness and significance, personalized presents are an excellent choice for demonstrating to a loved one how much you care about them.

Personalized presents can take the form of anything from a framed photo with a heartfelt inscription to a mug that has been customized with your significant other's favorite photograph or quote printed on it.

Additional possibilities include engraved jewelry, personalized keychains, and engraved writing instruments. You may also be creative and construct gifts at home, such as a scrapbook filled with images and notes or a personalized video montage.

It is essential to take into consideration the likes and interests of the person to whom you will be giving a personalized Valentine's Day gift in order to make the right choice. Consider an aspect of what makes them one of a kind and remarkable to the world. Make sure that anything you give them is something they will treasure, whether it be a snapshot of them from a memorable event or a meaningful quotation that speaks to them on some level.

When sharing personalized presents, it is essential to make sure that the gift is presented in a unique manner. This goes double for the exchange of the item itself. For instance, you might include a handwritten letter or message that came from the bottom of your heart with the gift, or you may present it in a unique box or bag. This will endow the present with an even greater sense of significance and uniqueness.

On Valentine's Day, exchanging personalized presents with someone you care about is a wonderful way to express your love and appreciation for them. In addition to this, it is an excellent approach to make them feel unique and express how much you care about them.

4. Take a Trip

Valentine's Day presents the ideal opportunity to spend quality time with the person you care about most by going on a trip together. A trip is an ideal way to commemorate your love and commitment to one another, regardless of the length of time you have spent together or the stage of your relationship.

If you're searching for something truly memorable, I highly recommend going on a beach vacation with your significant other. Take it easy and unwind on the beach, take a leisurely stroll in the evening, and take in the breathtaking view of the setting sun. You might also consider going on a scuba diving excursion, learning about the culture of the area, or taking a boat tour if you are feeling more daring.

If you are searching for something that is more opulent and romantic, you might want to think about taking a trip to one of the more romantic cities in the world, such as Paris or Rome. Spend some quality time with your significant other by going on a stroll down the Seine or discovering the ancient ruins of the Colosseum. Spend the evening with your significant other at a restaurant in the area, and then go out and discover the nightlife and culture of the city.

Regardless of where you decide to travel, be sure to organize some fun activities and events for the both of you to participate in while you're there. Try going out for a romantic meal at a restaurant in the area, enrolling in a cooking class together, or traveling to a new city together. Take a lot of pictures so that you can look back on them and recall your vacation.

No matter what you decide to do during the vacation, keep in mind that the most essential aspect of the trip is for the two of you to spend quality time with one another and appreciate the other's presence. Valentine's Day is the ideal occasion to commemorate the love you have for one another; therefore, you should make the most of this special day.

5. Prepare a Heartwarming Meal Together in the Kitchen

Valentine's Day is the ideal occasion for commemorating your love with a passionate supper that you and your significant other have prepared together in the kitchen. It is a wonderful opportunity to express your affection and gratitude for one another in a tangible way.

Begin the evening by establishing the tone for the evening. Turn on some music, light some candles, and make it into a warm and inviting space by doing these things. After that, get started on preparing the components of your dish. You have the option of following a classic recipe, or you can devise your own. Take the time to converse and joke while you are working together in the kitchen.

When it's time for dinner, make sure the table is ready with a gorgeous tablecloth and all of your go-to items. A toast with wine or champagne is an age-old tradition that never fails to wow. Have a good time chatting and laughing while you eat your food.

Following dinner, a sweet ending with your significant other can be a romantic dessert. It doesn't matter if you create something together or order it, but there will definitely be dessert at the end of the night.

Celebrating Valentine's Day by preparing a deliciously intimate supper for one another in the kitchen is a wonderful idea. It is an enjoyable way to express your love and admiration for one another, while at the same time creating a unique memory that the two of you can hold dear for many years to come.

Phase 2

Having taking time to execute the first 5 suggestions as explained in phase 1, its time to get to look at the remaining powerful and romantic 5 suggestions that would turn your valentine's day to a memorable one

6. Pamper Yourself at the Spa

Valentine's Day is the ideal occasion to convey to a special someone how much you cherish and value their presence in your life. To commemorate this one-of-a-kind day, why not surprise them with a relaxing day at a spa?

Spending precious time with your significant other while relaxing and being pampered at the same time makes a day at the spa the ideal way to spend valuable time together. You may get started by calling your neighborhood spa and making reservations for a couples massage package. This package will include a number of different facial treatments as well as massages that will help you relax.

Following your treatments, you have the option of unwinding in the sauna, the steam room, or the hot tub for a truly relaxing experience.

After you have had enough time to unwind and feel revitalized, you may have a memorable evening together in the spa's restaurant. In addition to the relaxing environment of the spa, you can indulge in one of the many delectable foods offered here. Following dinner, you are welcome to take a stroll through the garden and soak in the splendor of the natural world.

A night at the movies together is the perfect way to cap off a relaxing day at the spa. You and your significant other can put on an old movie, wrap yourselves in plush robes, and enjoy the experience together. You and your significant other are able to enjoy a warm and intimate evening together if you have some chocolates and champagne.

Spending Valentine's Day with the person you care about most by relaxing in a spa is a wonderful idea. It's the ideal activity for unwinding, getting back in touch with one another, and demonstrating your affection in a fresh and original way.

7. Visit a Museum

Spending Valentine's Day in a museum is a unique way to enjoy the holiday, and it would make a great celebration location. It is a chance to go over the museum's collection as well as participate in a variety of unique activities. A trip to a museum, whether it's one that's close by or one that you have to go to, is certain to make Valentine's Day even more memorable for you and your significant other.

To get the day started off right, take a leisurely stroll through the various galleries. Spend some time appreciating the artwork and learning about the stories that inspired the pieces. In the event that you are able to, look around the exhibits and ask inquiries. Discover something new and look for a piece of literature that moves you deeply.

If the museum is planning any activities in honor of Valentine's Day, you might want to consider taking part in them. Visitors can participate in a variety of engaging and instructive activities at many museums. Activities such as this could include guided tours, talks, or even activities including the creation of art.

Consider going on a treasure hunt with that particular someone if the two of you are in the mood for some excitement and adventure. Scavenger hunts with a Valentine's Day theme are offered at several museums to encourage visitors to explore the institution. It is a wonderful opportunity to get to know one another while exploring the museum together.

After you've finished exploring the museum, make your way to the restaurant for a memorable meal together. Many museums have cafes with wonderful and distinctive cuisine. Share in the pleasure of the meal together, and then reminisce about the incredible things you saw on your trip.

At a museum, spending Valentine's Day will undoubtedly be an unforgettable experience no matter what kind of festivities you choose to participate in. Participate in exciting activities, investigate the exhibits, and spend some time appreciating the works of art.

8. Sign Up for a Dance Class.

Taking a dancing lesson together with your significant other is the ideal way to celebrate love and passion on Valentine's Day, which is the ideal time to do it.

Dancing is a fun activity that allows you to express yourself creatively, raise your heart rate, and spend quality time with the person you care about the most. This Valentine's Day, you should be able to locate a dancing class that is ideal for you to take, no matter what level of experience you now hold in the dance world.

There is a large selection of beginning dancing lessons available for people who have never received formal dance training before. You can get your feet moving with simple movements like the waltz and the cha-cha, or you can try your hand at something a little more difficult like the salsa or the swing. If you already have some experience dancing, you should consider enrolling in an intermediate or advanced dance class so that you may improve your technique and learn some new steps.

It doesn't matter what kind of dance you take, you can always count on your dancing class to produce an enjoyable and passionate ambiance. You and your companion have the option of either learning together or practicing with each other during the breaks in the activity. Valentine's Day, it's a fantastic opportunity to relax in one another's company and rekindle the romance you once shared with your significant other.

At the conclusion of your session, you can celebrate your newfound dancing skills with a candlelit dinner for two or a night on the town. You can even take your practice to the next level by participating in a dancing competition that is held in your local area. You and your spouse will be able to get the most out of your Valentine's Day if you put in the effort to practice what you love and follow your heart.

9. Go Stargazing

Stargazing is a wonderful way to commemorate Valentine's Day, which is typically a day when partners spend time with one another. Gazing at the stars is a wonderful opportunity to appreciate the beauty of the night sky and to reestablish a connection with the natural world. In addition to this, it gives you a wonderful chance to interact with your spouse in a special and unusual way that will stay in both of your memories.

Visit a black sky park outside of the city if you want to get away from the bright lights of the city. These parks are located in distant places that have a low amount of light pollution, making them perfect for stargazing and observing planets.

If you want to have an experience that is truly one of a kind, you should look for a park that provides stargazing opportunities such as guided tours, telescopes, and other activities.

After you have selected a location, locate a comfortable place to lie down and observe the night sky. If you want to have a romantic evening outside, you should bring a blanket, a thermos full of hot chocolate, and your significant other. If you want to get a better look at the stars, you should carry either a telescope or a set of binoculars with you.

The night sky on Valentine's Day is jam-packed with stars and planets for you to investigate. Keep an eye out for familiar constellations such as the Big Dipper, the Belt of Orion, and the Pleiades. Remember to keep your eyes peeled for satellites and shooting stars as they move across the sky. You could even be able to get a glimpse of a meteor shower if you're lucky!

Celebrating Valentine's Day by going stargazing is the ideal way to spend the evening. It gives you the opportunity to appreciate the grandeur of the night sky while also giving you the chance to bond with your significant other.

This Valentine's Day, wrap yourself in a blanket, take your binoculars, and head outside to gaze at the stars!

10. Host a Night of Board Games

Valentine's Day is a special day for couples to celebrate their love for one another, but it can also be a terrific time for friends and family to come together and have some fun. The holiday is celebrated on February 14 each year. A night devoted to playing games together is often the ideal way to celebrate a holiday while also providing an opportunity for friendly rivalry.

Why not make the evening even more memorable by basing it around the holiday of love, Valentine's Day? You might make the game area more intimate by decorating it with symbols of love such as flowers, hearts, and candles. You might also serve some sweet goodies for the guests, such as chocolates and pastries shaped like hearts.

You may play some of the older board games like Monopoly and Trivial Pursuit, or you could play some of the newer party games like Exploding Kittens and Codenames to compete against each other. You might even pull out some of your favorite card games, such as Uno or Go Fish, and play those instead.

You are going to have a fun evening no matter what kind of game you play, so don't worry about that. Be sure you make the most of the opportunity by including some Valentine's Day elements, such as music, trivia questions about love, and unique rewards for the winners of the competition.

Valentine's Day can be celebrated in a fun and memorable manner by hosting a game night.

Conclusion

On Valentine's Day, loved ones take the opportunity to express their feelings for one another in front of their friends and family. You just need a little ingenuity and some careful preparation to make this already great day even more romantic. The 10 best ideas for a romantic Valentine's Day that are offered in this book will assist you in planning the ideal day for you and the person you care about the most. These ideas range from modest expressions of affection to elaborate surprises. You just need a little bit of planning and some work to turn this Valentine's Day into the most memorable and meaningful day of the entire year.

Valentine's Day is the ideal time to convey your feelings of affection to the person you spend the most time with. It doesn't matter if you're looking for a unique thing to do, a present to give, or a romantic gesture to make on Valentine's Day; there are lots of wonderful ideas that will make this year's celebration one that you won't forget. There is something for everyone, from intimate dinners to thoughtful gifts to memorable adventures, and everything in between.

You just need a little ingenuity and some extra work to make Valentine's Day memorable for the person you care about. Make it matter, and make it something you won't forget! Have fun!

Book description

This book is the best way to plan a romantic Valentine's Day for your significant other! It was written by Floyd B. Pung and provides ten excellent suggestions for making Valentine's Day memorable. This book is packed with innovative and one-of-a-kind ideas, including how to create a romantic evening at home, as well as how to prepare a romantic evening complete with candles, flowers, and music. This book offers all of the ideas that are excellent for a romantic Valentine's Day, whether it's a gift for your special someone, a romantic evening for two, or something unique and special. With the help of Floyd B. Pung's 10 Perfect Ideas for a Romantic Valentine's Day, you can turn this Valentine's Day into a magical and unforgettable experience for you and your significant other.